The Bloods

Also by D.S. Marriott

Incognegro
Hoodoo Voodoo

On Black Men
Haunted Life: Visual Culture and Black Modernity

D.S. Marriott

The Bloods

Shearsman Books

Published in the United Kingdom in 2011 by
Shearsman Books Ltd
58 Velwell Road
Exeter EX4 4LD

www.shearsman.com

ISBN 978-1-84861-151-1

Copyright © D.S. Marriott, 2011.

The right of D.S. Marriott to be identified as the author of this work
has been asserted by him in accordance with the
Copyrights, Designs and Patents Act of 1988.
All rights reserved.

Acknowledgements:

Earlier versions of some of these poems appeared in the
following journals and web journals:
*Blart, Signals, West Coast Line, Black Box Manifold,
The Notre Dame Review,* and *Hambone.*
I am grateful to all the editors concerned.

I am also grateful to Derek Murray, the Stephen Wirtz Gallery,
and Raymond Saunders.

Cover:
'Untitled (Jack Johnson Version 1)' (2008)
by Raymond Saunders

Contents

I

Lorem Ipsum / 11

II

The Virus Called Smith / 15
Black Sunlight / 17
Sirens / 18
Trueblood / 20
The Dog Enchanter / 21
The Oxford Serpent / 23
Greeking / 26

III

Hoerenjongetje / 31
Nothing's Left / 32
Acque Pericolose / 35
Rhapsode / 37
Venus as a Boy / 39
An Emblem Book / 43
Diglossia / 47

IV

Fish—Apostrophe / 51
Little Pip's Drowned Infinite Soul / 54
Pot Kettle Black / 55

V

Whittling, a Likeness Without Shade or Shadow / 61
Asyla / 66
White Phosphorus / 68
La Fierté de la Chair / 69
Child Boy Man / 71

The Loved One / 72
Willy Eckerslike / 74

VI

Nothing Precious Is Scorned / 77
Fields I / 80
The One Way Pendulum / 82
Teddy and Me / 83
The Red-Ribbed Ledges / 84
Into the Pit / 87
Orphans / 91

VII

Faros / 95
The Wolves (Acts I and II) / 98
The Bloods / 101
Newborn as Letter C / 103
Lakeshore, Trilce / 104
Soultracts / 107
Atlantis / 114

VIII

The Art of 000-3 / 119
Fields II / 121
Clash City Poets / 123
Riverflesh / 125
A Sequel / 127
Lester Young by Washington Square / 129

IX

Islanded / 133

Notes / 136

"Surely the blood-witness too belongs to the witnesses of truth.."
—Søren Kierkegaard, *Attack on Christendom*

"Blood is this absolute thirst."
—G.W.F. Hegel, *Encyclopaedia of the Human Sciences*

I

Lorem Ipsum

Looking at signs these days
    is all I can manage,
  the world adrift in glances
    as if so much flotsam & jetsam
is where it begins
  and what disturbs the eye is the line
    where boredom subsides
      beneath paneled ceilings.
        It is the ground
pywned because of a lifetime,
    when projects burn
      in thrall to new flames,
  and heads roll as if by magic,
      and the revolution feels cheap
because no longer immaculate (especially in summer),
    maybe because the intervals
        are now much longer, and the signs
  not so easy to read because, like most of us,
they sweat too. The red ones wink at me as I go past.
      Objects are not things.
Among the poplars
    the lynched body does not resemble
  an image. Only the other can save us,
    even though he wears funny peasant shoes
and walks like a German. In the cellar,
  a smell of mold and excrement,
and, in the obscure darkness,
the blackened and burnt stumps
of existence. Hard to forget the relief
    of not taking a bath,
  having just gotten reacquainted
    with the swarm inside my crotch.
  Things are not objects.
    I lie down in the rain,
      decked out in my tiredness,

    bound to what must be remembered,
what is absent.
    I reach out my hands but see nothing . . .
In a poem, silence sounds like a gunshot.
To the flame darkness is an offering,
                      in the moment
      just before something happens . . . .

II

The Virus Called Smith

Sometimes, at the end of a day,
the dream is of ashes in the yard.

A white dog
with sorrowful eyes,

hunting near parked cars.
Howling as if he'd never lived.

It's true.
The weather turns so quickly.

The cold that was meant
to be bracing,

is too delicate, and scorching—
a lesion upon the verge.

And the buckets
that we took from the reservoirs,

so dark, so fleeting,
that we had no fear—

hold nothing except lures.

☙

The thrust has taken us far—
from islands

of refused delusion,
to horizons rimmed by kerfs of snow.

Inside the matrix
that contains the all: a window with no views.

In the real world, after all,
each escapee falls, then wakes up

not far from a shingle shore.
Drunk and naked among nettles,

and wishing themselves home
after the hazy night before.

☙

Two servings
of rum vindaloo won't help us.

And the water
that we laved in handfuls,

now coils in the jars,
dirty, surreal, unknown.

There's no escaping it,
we're happiest when we drink alone.

When we turn to go back,
we take so many pills we open a magic door.

Agent Smith's tumbling eyelid
in plain sight, sunk in a single form.

Black Sunlight

From amid a grove of poplars it appears—and perhaps this testifies to how uninspiring the late morning walk had been—a little aspen tree, shimmering in the heat. It was not so long before this that he had set out, with his boxes and pencils, eager to do some drawing. The sun had been scalding, but despite the heat transfixing him, gouging his forehead, the dusty cart road had been easy underfoot, fringed by oaks and box scrubs. It wasn't long before he had come to a turn in the path and saw the tree: black, sickly, ancestral. By presenting itself in this way, close to the cattle wandering deep in the fields, straining to stand upright amid tightly spaced trees where shafts of light fell in a dense bluegreen, it was as if it were performing a courtesy for those passing through. And further, that it should form a stand in such a hot parched landscape suggested to him the most hopeful of signs—a circle of connection, a return. He decided to sit down and draw it. Beside him he placed a jug of water and a basket of strawberries. He felt content. Thoughts of restlessness abated; his mind grew rooted and still. It was as though something inside him were slowly uncoiling, wanting to burst forth into an act of pure attention. He felt himself recede into the present—as if hit by a sudden cold wave. As he begins to draw the tree seemed to arrange itself into an image of the eternity he craved rather than the brute emptiness he feared. But close up he saw something that clutches at his heart: something like a shadow, or a delayed pain, a gaze overflowing from the tree. He didn't know what to do with that ardour overflowing from a tree. Or that gaze. Think instead of a mind trembling under its own weight, trying to glimpse its own undoing; then subtract the feeling of something formless surging on the forested floor, waiting to flow back to the source. Or you could imagine that the tree itself, trying to resist the forces that shaped it, had burrowed back into this black earth. As though it had given up on its treeness—tired at last of its offices, unwilling to be woven from the earth. As though it had misread its own nature, refusing the illusion of its own form. He had engineered the encounter. He had wanted to see the tree free from artifice, whatever that may be. But it did not. It wanted nothing. Nothing at all. Better stop here. Better to simply stand, serving your purpose, waiting for the world to appear elsewhere.

Sirens

Then the rocks split and reformed,
a perfect mirror, us, the sea. The song
gone before each tortuous fold.
I taste the salt, the surf, the rime
that bore us to the rim of the world, the wind
as it cools into stone—
may we hear
the miracle of each splashing wave, the tides, the caves,
we princes
of the voids below.
It seems an age before it falls.
The only clue is Odysseus, his face blazing, now luminous:
his voice as stern as crystal.
It begins: the silences,
both yours and mine, the one without echo,
and the one heard by us all.
Surely wi must not
hear this name for the name-
less, with its dreadful recoil in the body, deaf as we fall
enchanted
onto rocks black with language?
But nosir, we would rather
bi stricken, rather suspek
(wutless the impervious ocean-I)
that each note carries traces of these islands,
that each riddim taps a nation, soundlessly in the wind,
that in surviving this hour,
we will wake
awed by the waves,
our voices masters, our speech no longer sold on, or mimicked.
All that is spoken
one love to ratted, as we resound in the dark caves—
the air on our lips, the echoes timeless,
the crisis of our mouths
deranged by a boum boum

inside a black hole gaping—
the infinities and molecules, decibels and watersheds
traversing us, our black cranial shells,
with our heads full of geometries,
our hearts full of coefficients,
and dark-brown gradients of our feet.

Trueblood

Nothing in the larder
but a drive-through Narnia;

a magic forest that you enter
from the wrong side;

oblivious to the fact
that here, too, you are fugitive.

At the thoroughfare a lion shouts 'no blacks'.
But your hormones say otherwise.

Better to follow the body to its ancestral end.
Ejaculate on the clockface.

Mouth gaping,
a queen leaks snow from every orifice.

From the rockpools,
beavers let out a rattling rebel yell.

The Dog Enchanter

What if he were to set off
panting through the ruins
swishing his tale
        over debris
mooching near the craters
the full-throated bark
deep inside the vertebrae
synchronized
        to the weak, the yielding—
his trick to know that 'ghost'
isn't the right word for
            scents
maundering his way
over the ragged ridgeline
where mines make effigies of sense
        and the universe presses in
pissing on the leafless trees:
        out there, see him return,
                where the dust
makes his tracks so easy to see
        as the journey opens before him
        his cry impending.
                Yes, see him return,
alert, muscularly alive, the good companion—
running on through the gorges and sleet
        running on and slowing
drawn to those found wandering in the valley
who don't yet know the meaning
        of the journey
their knowledge of time
        counseled by blood
as the ground rumbles from ricocheting shells
singeing his fur like hot bees—
why
        don't they condemn him?

rend him
        with strength and desire?
as he bears down on the laggards
stumbling in heavier snow
the ones who get lost in the shallows
              who give up
having nothing more to hang onto
who hand over their names when they see
the steam rising over the harnesses
the ghostfur burning in the lardcans:
why do
        they fall, awaiting him, mute
            with a surfeit of remorse?
Why don't
        they leap (with cynicism, with joy)
              from the drawn-out siege to the precipice?

As he steps into the light
between nature and innocence,
he is a dog who knows that refuge
        is always behind you,
and that absence from loss
is a pet seeking deliverance: stuff of dreams.

The Oxford Serpent

The not-yet readable
      text, not yet
uttered, still less
      experienced,
      with a flicker
                           sheds its skin in water,
                            the revocation
                        leaves a stain, a padel—

And you don't know why, secretly,
      the panicked mind
      should seek
            its rise
in such calamitous evolution

                            nor why the word
                            should take victory
                            from the shattered life

      amid the contractual fear
      of such shamed mediocrity?
But all those apple cores
speak
      of a peculiar reluctance to seed . . .
elsewhere the world listens in
to intense, multiple
      dreams of extinction
                            as the quagmire erupts—
            it's a book
            full of
            unworldly swamps
            and open ribs

                            and eve's urging:
                            the desiccation
                            of each letter

                              ringing through death
                                        and eternity,
            life's impossible flirtation
            with self-measuring actants.
            Drenched in the refusal
            the horizon turns its back.

Look—who is this unmade being
waiting to be milked?
Why does its mewling mouth
consume all grammar
when its speech is so corrupt?

            It is a fever-drenched bestial fear, and it is not. More enamel
                  needs to be extracted. Through the gaps ride
                  stallions making me hot, or is it absent?
                  And you're dying to say this,
                  harder and harder
                  as the black thing sheds its skin in water,
                  dispossessed of word, proof, context,
                  its origin lost
                  to a slavish heritage invented by remote.
                  Where he goes he knows that you will follow.

But the true other
is a nebula
of stretched plausibility,
        when all the statements issued
                should not be on the tongue.
The wronged not in words but in the desire

                        the barrenness
                        inhabited by
                        hostile dialects

the pages of the book
filled only by
tribal allegiance
and donnish
ennui.

Greeking

Sometimes a language—when it dies?—
wants not to be spoken any longer, wants reality ousted
from every syllable and sign, free
to name its former life. Sometimes,
in the midst of each echo, it will
hearken back to cooing, or even farther,
to the blank page, and inter itself
in its luminous weight, a dying still
looking for a world to name.
      The alphabet is *homo negro*
and erases every trace of my name. I've borrowed
its debt—letters, glyphs, scrolls
against doors, biblical tablets,
daubed slate, chalk. Talking,
as we always talked, not about reason
with its speech bubbles: sentences
obscure to sense, death, pain. Steps that lead
nowhere except to airports
papered over with books about flight. Beyond water
with its blue-black punctuation beneath
fraying charts of light. Garvey said
the thread is stronger than iron. We said
nothing is sewn. He said the secret sews
the possible. We said
the book remains untraced. Rabbi Jes said
the void makes him puke with boredom.
Everybody writes, taking the dialogues
to breathe more easily and enter the baths
with forgotten novels, discussing plot
and character, the never used pronouns, Ras's
invisible knights, and whether death exists
in each voice. We knew what this was—
a slashed name for weariness,
the concierge's posthumous annihilation, flesh
of the world. We sent our letters back to Jerusalem

and got back to work. And then, amid the pages,
syntax, weft, memes, no order or world. Suddenly the
illuminations burn, perish on the white page
with its pathos night after night.
Back then it was bizarre that,
after all that writing, we took sheaf from its trademark,
so inwardly gravitating to zero
beneath the stars. We were never lost.
Still later I think it makes sense that language should
lead back to death and silence
devote itself to the erased letters of the air,
a flight so inviolable it has little chance
of existing beyond the natural life of a poem.

III

Hoerenjongetje

Pull down the ledger: it opens like a glib,
the leather sweat-soaked
in its clinkered cubicle.

Be sure that your fingers
do not smudge the rills and flanks—
sand should not be strewn on paper already dirtied.

The writ should not be black from the sentence.
Loose the flaps but not your tongue.
Release the words from their trap,

but don't forget to nuance the meaning.
This is where true ownership begins.
A hand scratching worth from zero.

Nothing's Left

After Segismund
the remnants
have become thick with dust.
The wrack won't
be left behind, after all.

Someone has to rend with violence
the ruins,
the dead piled at the roadsides,
the fled villages pillaged
and burned.

Someone has to trudge
through sludge and snow,
through the livid brown smear
of an old shawl
on cratered ground.

Someone has to make legible
the shards, sleet and birds,
the angels hacked by windows,
the bleached tongues
possessed by the curious taste of gall.

Here we are, violent men,
moving like
water over bone,
riding between god and the world
on our journey home.

Our clan is 'Eldorado'.
We have suffered pain. No matter.
Our pleasures will take us
to other wars,
to other mistresses/ disciples of torture.

Segismund needs a brother,
and the dream that we are
a new illusion, too.
All disguises will be
torn to shreds, and the illusion of tearing.

Someone, a marionette or hireling,
will feel pure and shriven.
Someone else will remind him
of what it means to be alone.
The purity of submission as pure
as the insubstantial remnant
of life itself.

Others will call out
at the sidings, reminiscing
of how everything is in suspense,
joined together like syllables,
before they are hauled off to the camps.

There is nowhere for us to go
except exile. All the witnesses
have been locked up
with the taste of metal in their teeth.
Looking like actors
in a halfhearted theatre of shadows.

In their faces is a world
in whose dream
we exist if only for a moment,
because in make-believe
it is not always easy to tell
the dead who have gone
from the smell of someone burning.

Some say these are the sacraments.
Those who are truly awake
know that
light is but a purer darkness
thick and black
and settling over everything.
The future nothing but an ambush.
Let the bodies hanging from trees
make way for those
who are neither seen nor touched.
We are living proof
that everything fallen is falling still.

So what if we dream
of a king who wakes up ashamed,
mad as he goes, gun in hand,
down into the depths
with unopened eyes, his radiance
is oblivion made visible.

Someone has to clear away
the grass growing over
the gaping grey eyes,
join Segismund in his dreams,
outliving the desolate expanse of his vigil.

Acque Pericolose

He arrived in the city at night,
from a distance
it looked empty. The barbed wire fences
and burnt out cars,
and the sound of the wind
that is the sound of the mind falling,
a sound long awaited,
and hearing nothing
but the sound of the falls
that is the wind coursing through it, to eternity.
Whatever it was, the dark
held him motionless, unheralded,
oblivious to the drugs and the sex,
the false divinities,
the dead sleeping next to other men.
Like a star, he simply glowed
in the night as emergency crews
cordoned off the tenements
and darkness fell into darkness
beyond any familiar or wished-for destination.

The signs made him gag
because they make him spin,
but intoxication is no longer the enemy
and the ugliness of the world has no meaning,
a meaning which, if he had entered it,
would've placed him inside big blobs of greyness.
Today the unlived life begins.
He walks past iguanas
hanging from the fires. A drunk staggers past,
hauling three painted saints in a bin.
A dead dog lies black with flies
alone at this wonderful threshold
as if inflamed by the expiring, or the rush to expire.
Here the mind sees its likeness,

not in some grey zone,
but in some errant weightlessness
where each syllable carries the same piquant whiff—
figures stranded on moldering archipelagos,
and what is right and wrong befalls
the journey and the adage
like stowaways, new and unobserved, holding greasewet papers.

Who are these people
to have all this voluptuousness,
moving like locusts
between black fins of slag
and the wavering noise traffic
makes in cardboard slums—
for whom words do not exist, numbers do not exist,
emptiness exists? Universes cut to husks
in a yellow swag of hewed bones,
and whoever bleeds in the void will bleed forever
and whoever is abandoned will have *Clostridium difficile* as witness.
What self, for example, could possibly go there,
survive all that is said with effervescing laughter?
What gaze could follow such candour?
He went there, so they tell us, full of grace.
Recognizing the sweet
pleasures of having and being nothing, of not being saved:
scavenging where the veterans and crackheads are pegged.
He knew that he should not follow the feet of the faithful
through these hailstorms
and ferocious desert suns.
That he should quickly ride over these slums—
symbols of the purest disaster.
But he went there just the same.

Rhapsode

In a damp crawlspace, he said, no one can hear you,
the poets and translators are of no help. They
have grown bored of the jet-lagged soliloquies,
the irredentist theft. Words burrow like phantoms,
like clever remarks at a 3-star hotel. O croutons!
The dry heave as wastelands burst asunder
and the Lilliputian temples crack,
and somebody whispers: chaos
sleeps on your golden tongue.
Besides, the real terror is here,
the names dropped no longer
fall into the ears of princes,
as everyone knows save the modest Japanese.
The libations duly said I count
my money in my sleep. To whom
do I speak without giving answers,
to whom do I give in without pleas or demands?
I no longer scat-sing. I've tried being laden,
but my lederhosen caught on fire, and train rides
with the masses did not see them
beat their bloodied heads in grief.
    Married to words, divorced from posterity,
I pander ok?: but please don't tell the big guns
with their elegant *néant*. Luckily, there is no refuge
for my nerves, nowhere to be entombed.
I am the exquisite throwback. I will not be
shot in the head, like Lorca, and my little red notebook
will not cause libraries to burn. Property is theft
only for the loyal servant. The blacklists exist
only for those teetering on the brink of fate.
I know all this because of fiction
but can't seem to stop playing the Vaudeville dame.

The next morning as you disembark,
finally home after the vast continents & snow-covered territories,
women turn their heads, men burn
signs at the cemeteries, a one-legged man
runs behind you saying something strange and incomprehensible,
and children shout 'pedo pedo'
at you from across the tracks.
You know that there will be no triumph,
and no rendition of 'Parnassus, my Hokum'.
Just dirty laundry, and the invalid,
who has to move backwards through the gates.

Venus as a Boy

The whip, like the flesh,
is colour-coded—it crowns

the body as it folds,
exposes concealed bone—

(I watch) the blood pool
on the axis of the world.

There is no stand to take;
I will not, cannot,

shield him from harm—the boy
who, begging,

remains chained to the wall.
The only thing I can offer,

as usual, are words of love,
the dream of two bodies,

fucking, the thrust of obsidian
across the flame of his lips.

The boy, heaving,
says nothing at all,

his eyes grow dim
as pain scars, then they go out.

I carry the body,
naked, scrawny, streaked with blood,

walking slowly, as if in a dream—
waiting for the truth of a word.

When he first walked out of the woods,
like a god, shining,
the glow was like a shaping fire
and, inside it,
the ceremonies of air swooned,
as night, undone,
staggered back reeling from the radiance.

All who saw him wanted him,
but all were soon disturbed
—ruined—
by his beauty,
terrified by the forced choice.
Like them
I too wanted to murder, rend,
struck dumb by cruelty.

Our hungers fed,
wanting to suck in the flesh
until gagging
on the entrails in our mouths.
Life grew round the juices
as each, swallowing,
reaped
the innermost, lying inside him,
without hope of recovery
and, whatever else,
prepared to follow on.

But then the miracle came. No one spoke.
On his eyelids
appeared a darkening crown
of gold. His body
changed from black to gold, from flesh to icon—
as if the outward guise

had miraculously chosen to robe itself
in a power not its own;
as if gold had become flesh here, at this time,
to gather up all the heart skipping moments
into one priceless assembly,
the flowing made hard,
the body astonished, petrified.

Against this longing made visible
this demise,
I tried to remain
indifferent, or calm. I failed miserably.
Did I love him?
Gold became his memorialization, his catastrophe;
and where he made himself a path
I could only look on, bewildered.

Beauty had made him impassable, scalding.
Even when the sunken cheeks
streaked black with blood
dripped gold onto the stems and the terraces,
I could only think of my rage,
then of my shame.
I walked away when my own voice failed me.

The gold was there from the beginning,
it was the one thing that separated
him from the torturers and seducers,
from the free and the enslaved.
For without this thing—his love—
none of us could reflect back
the heat from the fire,
nor release the evil from this exquisite thirst.

And, yes,
he followed the path to its end,
he was obliged to, for there was
no escaping the greater violence.
He had no rights, only wrongs.
The singular suffering of a boy,
 whipped because he had no flaw to offer, or condone.

An Emblem Book

"Pondus meum amor meus; eo feror, quocunque feror"
Augustine, *Confessions*

This emblem, your last, is where your body lay, cold and black in the rain. In you the world shrinks down to one harmonious core: five notes the only warrant.

And so in the morning, at first grey light, you walk out to the border, where a stray overtakes you, and stops, studying you. You look down at your shoeless feet and mumble something. And what one sees here, in the first light, to the right of the tow road, stretching out to the blankness, is the frontier... You walk towards it, you and the stray little islands of understanding, but when you look back the dog has gone, there's the feeling of utter tiredness, and music itself feels like pleasure without hope, as if everything were about to stop.

☙

In retrospect, those years in the Soviet Union were almost paradise: the applause of crowds raining down in the nameless dark: and, seated in the darkness, turned away from the applause, the wires strung from black sagging hands. The onset like an apparition, but when you first walked through the plush rooms it was like travelling blind with your back to the wind. You stood looking out through the tall enormous windows and had to remind yourself that everything was ok. Even the birdsong sounded like a deep ache echoing from far away. And in the mirrors, on the pillows, wrapped in blankets, is the sense that all the links have been lost, that everything has been shorn away, unable to sleep because the nights are endless. An iron bed next to the window and a new set of clothes after you cut your wrists. Each day Lenin's statue made its way to the barricades, and, without believing, you marveled at the churches and factories ousted by poetry. You held on tight to the taxi doors as the ambulances sped by and, for almost thirty months, survived the smokefilled speeches bereft of metaphor. You, the poet of bar rooms and courtyards, beloved by party officials dazzled by your reign, who kissed your cock from the dormant pits of their appetites. You, the deliverer of speeches, standing frozen in doorways as words grieved at the mere mention of your name. Everything that you were uncoupled from its mooring. And yes, in your madness, you heard the dead stir, whispering under the sheets like departing lovers.

༄

At the crossing the railcars pass by with a shimmer, like mist passing between two panes of glass. You try to remember your hopes as a child, climbing onto the windowsill looking out to the garden, wanting to slide down the depths of unknowing without guilt or hesitation, each day shaped as if you were the heroic Moor. Playing the boy spied behind the mirror. The gargoyle, its maternal fiction, had to be slain. What did it matter if you played the mute role, the tormented hen? Hidden behind all that pretend-childlikeness was a body opening, no longer pliant; all one needed to do was stretch the grin until it fitted the mask. Walk and talk differently on the boards. Become (almost) identical. Was it the lights or were your eyes playing tricks on you? Since it didn't matter, you rose and unwrapped the tokens, waxed your whole body black, and used European art to tighten the meshing (and suture, as it were, a new black blueprint). Kissing the bone was, you understood, what happens when the only vogue is greasepaint *or* negro. Pretending to step through the frame you held on tight to the reins, quietly filling your coat with great deeds of longing. Surprised to find yourself exposed to all that absence. After all, a lie isn't a mirror and a lover in the dark is not a reckoning. You took great strides to redeem the loss, and mimed all the mimes: juggled every sin and ledger, sober and dark as a bootblack or a returning soldier—yes, you bathed in the cheers, never wondering why the thousand eyes on your back became a thousand eyes spellbound by your power. Half-awake, you played to some other audience; and when the show was over your afterimage hangs in the air like a death. Or a continuous shattering scream. We gave in to it like a montage of the inadmissible. Eyes closed, voice soaring.

༄

A shadow in the sky. It took you two days to cross the environs of the city, scribing the concrete sweeps until later, near the patrol booths, the interstate feels like an empty name. It began to snow: the grey flakes descend in a spiral of expiration as you trudge on through the sodden drifts. And as you watch them you realize, even the deniers have blind faith. The cold doesn't bother you, but something else buzzes in your blood. A kind of gift, or imagining. And so when you walk out to the road with two empty suitcases, stopping only by the river to consider the running waters, a great gulf of nonexistence descends plunging you into nothing, waters in which your own image gradually dissolves, as of snow: and you are proud of it, too, this abandoning that is the opposite of compassion, this loss that is the first falling of snow. The five notes are now fused inseparably with a thousand voices, voices that don't sound like you, but rather like waters rising, the banks overflowing. Out of which you fashion a truth. The Party, as usual, hides the discovery behind a veil of resignation, but only then do you sing without a wobble, or a pause. Or was it simply because you'd already weighed up the pros and cons during those radio performances, the great sludge of syllables falling out of the calcified pain of your mouth?

༄

You walk on. You keep a constant watch behind you because the near future is one in which not much of you remains. Here in the draws the tracks of the railroad are not as bleak as at the frontier. The only thing that moves in the streets, that exists and is real, is the absolute. It claims you; and your memory of it forces you to just stand there, waiting . . . .

You just stood there. The room was empty. The pictures gone from the walls, the last rows set beneath a window of Mannerist illusionism. The greysuited men speak with the voices of former lovers. They call your trial the *advent*, you let the inquisitorial *as if* fall from your shoulders as if you were another character—the charred liver of patriot, dissident, communist, the cerebral appearance of liar, lunatic, thief. Now the truths proposed by truths feel like the prison of old age. The galleries stacked all the way to the border. Even so, you hurt yourself—how does one explain the intervention? the need to offer confession, to accept the trap, to take up arms against oneself—as if fidelity were no more than a conspiracy carelessly left behind in an abandoned bunker. Sometimes they play your records on the radio but music for you is now not even a memory. The five notes are now a list of names: the last symbols of the collective, *or anything that's not you, nor could ever be.* The records are over, but poetry remains: in the night it sounds like a child singing on the radio next door. Then, wrapped up in blankets, shivering with old age, you turn to it and hear a kind of music that is hope echoing behind a descending veil. No trace of scale in this attention. No token for the heartthreads hanging there unpicked vein by vein.

Diglossia

Then someone says let's go—small chunks
of time instantly duplicate themselves
with brutal honesty (the moment when
obsolescence converts the depopulated city)
and cuts to the chase blurs into deep sepia
at the outskirts near the dried-up well
where metaphors used to plunge deep in
the unintelligible depths the rain falling steadily
on the rusting junk where you used to drop
your trousers at the far shore of the sluices
and at the edge of it my oft-repeated thought
hobbling along with the most abject inflection
that we should avoid the swans nesting there:
oh to be a child again, dying without knowing it,
the dark so very quiet because ephemeral
and the void a stench almost too solid to touch—
to this life, not worth the loss even as we reach it,
where we are led, like beasts, partakers of a composed end,
hunched and shouldered and generally mute,
truth no less feigned because embodied
where I smile or blush at your unwitnessed parts—
      why do things
become words only to shudder in the embrace
bared by a comfortless reminder of resemblance?

IV

Fish—Apostrophe

"the black and merciless things that are behind great possessions"
—Henry James, *The Ivory Tower*

At night, when I wake up at night, choked with anguish, the Moors leave their drawings outside my window. I let my eyes rest on their dark faces before slowly following the chasms and the troughs of each picture. Clearly something is coming full circle, but I only want to see it from a distance. It is quiet as I stand watching the straw-red lips of a child, perilously perfect, surrounded by darkness. The world will choke me before this image fades. It rises sheer with a thrashing force. Time reels from the impact.

☙

Something has run its course but this moment is only the beginning. It is too dark to see anything but the image. I walk sightless towards the window with my hands out held in the cold. Suddenly something dense appears shuddering out of the darkness like a weight on a trawl line or marker rolling in the flux, something left behind, and in its wake, past disbelieving, I give up trying to find out what. What is there to hide? Some ancient corpse that I have improperly eased out before offloading? Some black remnant that I can't look at anymore? I've never sought refuge from any image. Indeed, they've absorbed me. This is a lie. I have entered an irreality beyond which there is nothing. Then something catches my eye as I move slowly through the dark. The edge of the negative shows visible like a weir stone, it is part of the image seen floating like a ghost. Look at it. In the historic clutter of my attic, I study this: simple, naked, exposed.

☙

I am in the world. Whereplace else? Another world in which I hold the pencil over the paper as if it were a pinpoint on the karst and each line is the pure name of *terra nullius*? Who do these arabs think I am, walking amid these bleak and barren landscapes, squatting down and looking at these blurred forms written in the sand? I have my metaphors, my patio, my books, my leafless trees, and every night, without exception, my waking terror. No more—the strain and effort is causing me to smear what is already a blur, descending toward the edge of light as a lentor. Here melancholy slips away into recollection. But more is required. What? How else should I approach the fog enveloping the image of this child whose innocence is as evil as it is pure? Drowning in the depths radiating from the whited out blinds of his eyes and, as I now descend, astonished at the unmanageable heaviness of the Moors?

☙

What age the child? I want to lie down for a moment but I can't budge. There is a vast ocean beneath me chilling me with its power and intensity, and hovering near the surface, soon to burst forward or sink back into the depths, biting and tugging and dragging me down into the black fume, are nameless things that I see without believing, filthy, vile, rotting things that are coming to steal my eyes, causing a sound to escape my lips that is more anguish than animal. As if I had heard myself screaming through the water after being pulled down into the dark.

☙

Why a picture? Why *this* picture? Reflecting nothing but myself. A nothing I cannot speak of because there, lying in the waves, going slowly down, right at the heart of what pours forth, are the Moors. Imagine watching a ship founder in the gathering storm, the dead and the dying thrown into the menstrual blush of the ocean without hope or sound. Each word perishable, unbreathable, waiting to fill the swollen and discoloured lungs of the drowned. There is nothing I can do but look on because here the heart is all on the eyes of fishes now, but its slavery now is much colder.

☙

The memory consists of a child, barely grown, speaking Arabic. There is someone else, a boy. There are the parents. Who are dead. The memory is his alone, and for good reason. As he looks at the drawing he wanders would he sacrifice himself to the boy as the boy does to this drawing? The question that plagued him and never made it into words but which filled him with ardent desire for, and devotion to, the other's art, was this: the stench of corruption that disfigures the world was spellbinding to him, but was the scent also his, and precisely because of his innocence? He lies down in the darkness. The silence is absolute. This very thing that haunts him is not death but an absence of punctuation. The dark closes in.

Little Pip's Drowned Infinite Soul

The sea is filled with wreckage.
Adrift, I grow in weight.
You must understand
I was never helpless.
Even a small boat
must pass through the dark swale
to return to the cold beaches.

Pot Kettle Black

This 'play' has 3 short scenes, each with its own title. The stage is littered with lampchops and knives. At the front of the stage there is a brightly lit commode with the word 'poetry' on it. To the left are three chairs. On one sits the poet, Breadfruit, on the other, the poet, Saltfish, and on the third, the poet, Cricket Pitch.

Breadfruit
>When it is late, and the rabble downstairs
>spinning turntables, leaves you
>shoving wax into your skull,
>listen to your white goods, never evacuated
>and constantly humming in the empty kitchen
>ready to submit unflinchingly to the blitz.
>That human stain, it works its way
>across each immaculate floorboard to the garden,
>imperiously gathers itself in pools of no surrender
>and deep shagpile colonies,
>the purewhite interior in the empire of no setting sun.

Saltfish
>In those days
>every moment was a darkie
>and every hour bloodied rivers of bloody wogs.
>A coupon became snakes just after
>your winnings.
>Georgie with the firelights, lit
>the dead ships of the future
>(the only thing he owns
>is the past), where his mother slept
>by the overhanging orange trees, in whose ripeness
>death smelled,
>the green logs breathing the exultant words
>where she lay dozing.

Sometimes, if you sang
an orphaned syllable, the streets would erupt
in harmonicas, nostalgia, bare feet,
and men would razor the sweetness
from their teeth. One
became a man by returning to oneself
what had been taken in the long war.
The wutless would wave flags, then,
cutting white with abandon
embarrassed by rum without snow, disya,
the names of the people forgotten.
The only words that matter are words
left elsewhere.
Let the rain drink doubles—the factories sweep
the ditches, the trains
walk barefoot in your memory,
while the image of you, savage
as a seed on a voyage (it opens onto
a game of lost thoughts and tragedy), still
sprouts its great black stem
for what has been dreamed
with hatred or impotence.

Cricket Pitch

    That things should be cold and clear
like crystal, and words
salt the icy paths of remembering. Islands
the frozen carcasses of insects. Wi nah sayit
the black suspiration of each breath
shimmering in a forsaken yard (a crib,
a dark nest for each shadow), then zeros
black drops of blood. Islands. Time
is now whiskey and stout, growing cold as the cornmeal soup
on the stove. Abide with me,
but the world is no longer made of oceans,

and the lesson of *Windrush*? Don't look back.
My parents turned into meridians—why?
Because they saw the snow
and didn't know it was a state of mind?
When the hail fell, the known world
became a secret door, gaping. My father thought
airplanes were pyramids of the mind
regions of impossible blueness. Only birds
went there. Now he too falls from the sky.
Airplanes, like the ocean's currents, bound
to hours and minutes: exile, silence,
just one of many songs you can hear.
And behind the boardinghouses the smell
of tripe on the air, the faces locked
in ration books and rain, the coasts
ringed with brown, awash
with imperial romance. And lampchops? I say it's
not some duel between punk and rastafarian,
but gestures that belong to no one,
boats underneath the firing, a song
from which there is no verdict. If there is a choice,
let's say it's not *what to imitate*,
but how to speak the undamaged word. How?
When the housemaid draws the curtain
and she knows we know she has life beyond the window,
the sudden darkness is still shocking
as the image and its wreckage
disappears from view. Losing
remains a black verb.

V

Whittling, a Likeness
Without Shade or Shadow

What *can* be shown *cannot* be said.
—Wittgenstein, *Tractatus Logico-Philosophicus*

He knew that his time had come. Things and their likenesses fell like shadows over the city, waves collapsed like mountains, and rain clouds blotted out the sun. He walked through the streets wrapped in his filthy frockcoat. He held the shackles at his waist and held the slave by the hand. At the farther edge of the town they came upon a flock of gulls, nesting close by the ports as the rain came on, darkly, over the pavilions. The slave chased after them as they whirl away, a single blur of motion. At the quayside they saw an abandoned fishing boat. A corpse floated by in the water as the tide slapped along the jetty, the outcrops rimmed by trash and excrement. They stood and watched the pooling water, their shoes damp with fishscale and mud.

The visible world was no longer his dominion. He had plundered everything from brink to rim. It was a hard hand he cast. Memory of the crossing like an impassable chasm he could not escape from. For a brief moment he saw the sea open its jaws. A charred ruin. As if a sun had fallen, burning in the water. Not even lightning could extinguish it. Such visions he knew come but once in a single guise. They wreathe the life and blind the eyes and arrest all sensibility. From them no answer comes nor is any expected. Like a splinter retained and in no sense lifted, such collisions throw the known world into disarray, beggar time and soul the most completely.

The storm had left the port ransacked. They sat by the side of the road and ate the last of their provisions. They wrap up their bundles and set out upon the road again, cold and shivering and trying to get their bearings in the twilight. The gulls return through the coastal mists, a raucous blur. As they veer past he hears a kind of cadenced longing hovering on the edge of his inner ear. A thread that they respin retrace together. He wasn't sure what it was about the slave but he felt protected by him. With his great staring eyes he looked like a totem or idol. In his long silences there was ruin and desolation, yes, but also poetry. In the nights sometimes he'd wake and hear the slave singing softly. The words meant nothing. Or perhaps nothing is what defines him; he simply burns, glorious like a lightning-seer. When the man looks up at the dirty night sky he has to suppress a maddening desire not to laugh; in between the grimy streets and the filthy blankets there is no meridian and no fall, however fortunate. He knew that the world wasn't anything like he saw it, and even less like he painted it: the storm that surrounds them no light can penetrate, no light can illumine. They walk down to the quay with a touch of salt in the air. They watch the flop of unhooked fish on the decks. With their mouths open they look like supplicants who have lost their way. Terrified by all around them.

⁂

The painting shows a girl turning her head away slowly, methodically, disdainfully, the blood livid from the slap on her cheek. There is a look in her eyes both ardent and ferocious as she turns away from him at the mastrails. Crossing the deck he felt that he should not have hit her so hard. The crew were watching him, excited by this violence. He couldn't speak. Imagine the surprise of a toy musket popping for one brief moment only, imagine the sound gathering, secretly, then approaching the disbelieving I with the roar of its impact. The sound opens a hole in existence, breaking like waves in the mind. Why had he not stopped himself? Why was his mind betraying him? He walked back towards her and punched her till she sank. She made a hollow moaning sound. He was tired. He rested against the guardrail, holding her chains, then he yanked her up and began beating her again. Everything in the painting is bathed deep red. The maps and ropes. Canvas and boxes. The dark corked barrels, tins and shot. He stepped back and looked at his work. On the girl's face he saw fear and pain. He knew what would happen to her. So few years old. He bent to his work again. When he looked up he noticed that the rivets had broken and the mast had cracked, and that there were rents running down into the depths of the hold. Then he noticed the sea. The dark leaden sea. Is he ready to embrace the storm he has created? I'm sorry, he said. I'm sorry.

During his early years we know that, from the beginning, what he wanted to do was to travel the frontier between objects seen and the violent and illicit nature of what shines forth, the origin of law. Life was not something to be *shown*, an effigy of a world made perfectible. No, life was the work of absolute truth. There were times when he sat watching the slave that he began to worry about the things he had hoarded but he knew his work wasn't about greed. He wasn't sure what it was about but he thought it was not about plunder or the money on the tables. It was not a question of wanting or of not wanting, but of fear and impatience. The fear that the world would always outdo the borrowing, and that the nausea he felt would bear down with a verifying force, his eye unable to behold it. As for the critics, he so despised the words falling out of their mouths that he avoided, when he could, their tiresome acquaintance.

☙

They were a long time finding shelter from the rain. Their blankets and coats were soaked through and hung heavy with water. He put the coats and the bundles beside the door and beckoned the slave to unlace his boots and pull them off. He began to think that there was no hope of rescue, nor will there ever be. He pinned a sheet of paper to the whitewashed wall. He stood back. He leaned down and kissed the slave. The slave looked down. Don't you like my epitaph, he said. He walked over to the paper. Then he drew a line, erased it, then went over it again, and then threw down the brush in a temper. Better to drown a slave than reign in heaven, eh lad? He went to where his things laid then he scooped up his boots and handed them to the slave. He trudged out through the downpour leaving the slave to gather up the bundles. The slave took one last look back at the picture and then followed him out to the road. The man stopped and looked about. The rain had slowed and the houses with their crested roofs looked stripped and ravaged in the greying landscape. In the sleet he saw the darkness of many forms; the eyes of the dead showed through each image. He'd little idea where he was and he thought that the boats had slipped their moorings. Look, he said. The slave turned and saw children watching them, their feet sunk in the rising shit waters. They went on. They set off through fields drenched by rain. In the silence gulls called out to them as they trudged past. It's evening as they leave the city. The sky is filled with great sheets of flame. In the wooded outskirts he thinks that he remembers the slapped face of the slave girl, but the meridian lies elsewhere, in between some other world and some unimaginable future.

༄

Perhaps in Slavers the illusion pursued is not that of history but in how paint surrenders to the surface. There is nothing to see, really, but a sense of anticipation left dangling like a leg in the sea; even if we see some kind of halo from the eye looking out, invisibly, into the whiteness of an absolute, into the marrowed folds of clouds sweeping away to the east, what shows forth is not the world but the eye centered on the obscure mirroring of itself, the painting neither truth nor counterfeit but its own form of representation, sunlashed and purple, stained by rain. And what did he see? Bursting out through the frame, rising from under great swathes of foam, are monstrous fishes and sharks. Which is to say: what he saw, as they cleave, are metaphors of life as infinite war, a murdering in which there is no holding back, and no reserve. What we are left with is the refusal and the ecstatic suffering—he would have willingly put out his eyes for such a look—the voices echoing off the stern, the lower decks flooded.

༄

They climbed the crest of a ridge and set off through the drifted fields until they came to a river. No movement no sign of life. They knelt down and drank. After a while the man sat back and closed his eyes. Are you okay? he said. The slave nodded and sat down wordlessly beside him. The man was lost in contemplation. There was something in the life of a slave he thought, something similar to what the world owed him, a world that had forced him to wallow in spectacle and evocation. As he looks out over the hills to the sea, he thought about the power of imitation, but he didn't know that behind him the slave too was concentrating on creating a new form. He'd been cautious, watchful, but all the while he'd been learning how to shape the junk and miscellaneous things scattered all about them into new forms. And so, little by little, his dreams had started to encroach upon the waking world. They sat in the darkness. It was total and consuming.

The man tried to make out the tree branches but the sight exhausted him. Where are you, he said. The slave didn't answer him. The dark, like the silences, belonged to him, they could not be plundered even if he was unable to complete his side of the bargain. The *said could not be seen*; the dark could not be spoken. This he knew as he got up and turned to where the man lay before he headed southwards. He heard him losing his temper with him, but he carried on walking into the woods. Talk to me, the man said, but he would not. He looked back to where the voice had come from. Then he set out through the woods again. He could see no worse with his eyes shut. He thought he heard birds. If the moon went out, there would always be this light that feels unceasing, flickering below the flight of gulls climbing, on divergent paths, over blackened fields. Walking beneath the grey sky, knowing that ash is a reprieve from an even greater fire; is it any wonder then that he hardly has any strength left over for the dark unfolding, nor time for the painter whose fixed price condemns him?

Asyla

The bible salesman looks familiar
—I'm thinking of buying Deuteronomy and Ruth,
or maybe Exodus and Genesis,
its been such a long time
that I don't remember
the plot—
he has a lived-in,
extremely close-shaved face.
I don't know him.
He gave each of us discounts
for different reasons
for knowing the score.
I went to buy Revelations
but he said I had vision aplenty.
Looking for the index
I happened to see the holy ghost: the year of my grace,
but the watchword was I'se a muggin...
Then
I understood.

In my apartment block there is a Mexican who crucifies himself every Friday at 8. I did not choose this, he says. Nor did I not choose it. There is no key to his door and no balcony from which he can escape. I have just been informed that he is always late and enjoys being stuck in traffic. Next door to me lives a Russian—Tom: he rents, he visits the cemetery every day. Just in case, he says, the hereafter is already here. Every evening the city lies shipwrecked in banks of yellow fog. Time melts away into thin air and sometimes you can see it diminishing. You can't escape it, Tom says, scanning the horizon. The irrevocable will happen: the Leviathan will shed himself in the four quarters like a veil: and we will all strip-mine the moment for souvenirs. Then everyone will say you'se a ho as he rises from the waves, the words whispered as if behind arras, disbelief the pure essence of the state, happy over our ability to look on the deeps beaming with blood and not be afraid. I've never been on vacation. My time is no more mine than my word. The complainer—the bible salesman—is demanding that I return Joshua and Kings because my check will not clear.

Sorrow cascades (into the building)....................the present is too late (the Mexican): this resurrection, a peculiar perversion of what was or will be, cannot be taken through the eye of a needle, nor be thrust out of the lobby, and, apparently, everyone is demanding to know who is sleeping with this year's star.

White Phosphorus

against the raw
unflinching state

    a war without any meta-
    physical jurisdiction

    I mean
    when it looks as if everyone
    (the flesh seared
    beyond flesh)
    are wearing
    ill-fitting coats made of ashes

        and the condemned houses
        crumble
        into sewers

and the most
you can handle
are yesterday's pleasures

        scraped raw
        by dying and the fear of dying

        as a particularly white drizzle
        begins to fall

the cheering of the righteous
can be heard in Jerusalem

          where you enjoy the earth
          being heaped over you

La fierté de la chair

The hills that are the corrosole's secret
sidle up to mountains like whores
until the ash reabsorbs them. There,
one day, we cut our eyes with blades,
our skin, more dry than the black veins
of sand – buried amid the fertile warmth of caves
as in the days when we drank breastmilk at the quayside.

Now that the ocean has lashed the lava's
deep fronds making them ageless
at the coastline, all around someone has hung
on the limbs of lianas insects that sting
along the path that goes down
to where the three roads meet;
insects whose eyes have dried out
and are no longer cold to the touch; and over the rims
the thick blue meniscus of the tam tam shrieks
and shatters the pedestal name of the dew
where we walk through rows of cane, bush, loa.

    More than the hurricane's streaming eye
in the whirlpools that expose us, the jungle
leaps from paradise onto swamps: and still it breathes
in us, that black fathermilk which one day we drank, licking
it from our lips. Among the ferns that bind
one branch to another, the heart struggles
like newly hatched larvae
caught out on the dry plains and rivers;
and sundried and gaping it sickens,
sweating the last drops of a malnourished voyage.

Thus maybe the dead too are trying to find their way
back to port; their eyes coals more pitiless
than tight round diamonds, and all around
(graves swallowed by a murderous whinnying foam)

black snakes crawl through each vein, scoop
out the thin skulls
as if they were vessels;
and their white plumes brush by us even now,
like white horses churning black foam, so close still,
and sink back in the gulf of oblivion and drown ....

In memory of Aimé Césaire

Child Boy Man

Strange that nobody notices
when it starts raining
my mouth melts into a dark pool
of iridescent glass.

I am the boy from the green cabaret, but no one knows it,
the story I tell is more secret
and more true (like a picture),
and I wish to speak it
with my entire being.

An idea flashes across my mind
that things are moving farther away
as if seen through a distant lens, each moment so transparent
they seem strung on a crystal.

When it starts raining,
it's impossible not to want to see the shifting shoals
the running blue-black surge of knotted string
sprouting in every little crevice. Dazzlingly illegible.

I'd like to walk back to the shore.
Watch them move closer, in,
lifted, like Moses, beyond themselves,
ignorant of the clumps of soil, leaves, detritus.

For a long, long time
I walked the length of the road.
Imagine their (my) surprise
when men & women slowly fade in the dark mist.
A white dog runs on the beach making it whiter.

The Loved One

And so it goes on: the ritual hand no wafer
passed down from boy to boy a wager dating from birth
like a new myth written for light relief
inside the first kiss first blush first happiness.

What a painful movie the ritual is it suddenly recalls a blue black screen
far away—
through the eye of a needle
the opiate of a frenzied suck—
you sing, undress
towards what paradise and what forgetfulness.

The priest says how marvelous virtue is
Oh his hand on
the peculiar perversion of memory
let nothing end that nothing begins!

My great-grandpa jumps through the psalms
the beaches that he strips for
swimming off for the new eden
on the scorched grass the dead haunt for me.

It's not so much that all fields are battlefields
where the innocent are sacrificed
and only monsters receive gifts—
only what destroys us can truly be loved.

The unknown martyr has lost its luster
heart and soul tidy away virtue and wool scarves
a mirror what padre kisses ass to mouth
not a single bird is left to eat its bitter crust.

He's swallowing the heavy ritual made of memory and passion fruit.
Here he sits an unforgiven man
riding his last train home

shadows on his dark face
haunted by the grief of having been born.

Farewell old friend
I'll enjoy eating your cancer for dinner the ash in the throat.
(Imagine an angel buried without testicles or eyes.)

And so it goes on: know that
I was condemned the moment the wings swept over me
vomiting green-backed poems
over the starlit pavements like some rich vintage
a yen for poetry's inner emptiness.
In any case it's hard even to know how far poems should go.

Oh my, the self-righteous are stifling!
And it seems the snuff movie is little more than atheism.
Let us fall into its lethargic handsome arms
face-to-face with the lived-in deception
the junk-marks and already neglected snow
like boggery beneath some daft grinning padre.

Willy Eckerslike

Saturday morning.
An invisible procession of divas passes by—
voices without names—
slipping on the snow eager to degrade themselves.

Listening while tipsy, with effort—
the flakes of newky brown
carried on rivers of courage—
to the voices, breathless.

I ought to get up,
slip into my trousers, get some water:
Don't fool yourself, they say,
you too will have to degrade yourself.

When you say goodbye
to the voices you are losing.

VI

Nothing Precious Is Scorned

1

December morning. It began with the cold pinch of winter, when the first chill fell on the clay of the cabins, and the thinnest shadows fell to earth as black ice swam across the eye of the lake and the dying sound of leaves fell into thoughts left frozen.

Perhaps it was the long pall that drew him, so early in the evening as he walked out into the chill air, perhaps it was the fast hardening ice thwarting his advance that spelled him as smoke tightened under foot and, cloudless, the night gave fullness to his waiting, watched by the animals as he mounted his horse. As he rides towards the cabins there is blood in his thoughts, a desperate wish to earn his spurs. The first time he raped her he said it was like banging his stick against multiple doors, or like pouring milk onto a black headstone. In any case, she was merely an ornament, a husk, an emptiness to be molded by force. Perhaps this is why he leaves her banged up and stammering into the night air, her mouth shattered, her body crushed and bleeding, her inner life become a thing of being. Perhaps this is why she weaves for him a dark cloth of bitterness where all that is torn trails mutely, a riddle that she trails from dusk to evening, a purl which she spins and unwinds with a voice no longer that of a girl. *The spun precarious weaves, secrets that she weaves for him alone.*

Days of oblivion, of uneasiness followed. Of separation, too. They looked at each other without a word. What could they say? They could only resist, only retreat into their difference. As a youth he had had nothing to lean against, nothing to rest on, he had felt orphaned in the fullest sense of the term, absent from himself, without weight, or reverberation, without hope. Now when he spoke it was with a master's voice, the semes landmarks of engendering. The keys lay in force. The morning after he tastes its privilege, and would swallow it if he could, but his vows mean that he doesn't have to. This only compounds the cruelty. After such bitterness, is it any wonder she should seek to reenter the warm baths of nonexistence? Imagine nothing and in the middle of nothing a brief shadow. What if you were told this tiny opacity is you? Without rights and protections, without childhood, without past, chained to the absence of being, your being a stone. *No one can lose more than the slave loses*; it is a loss molded by violence as the inner life drains away. But what is force? It is an act in which all are implicated, but the force of that 'all', as of the implication, remains uncertain. And not everyone is equal to its weight.

2

With these black threads that pass through her fingers she unravels the world. With each spool she unwinds all that she has ever been and all that she was allowed to be. She spins loss after loss. Seated in darkness, turned away from the night whose stars mirror the work of her hands, she sews unseeingly, weaves the cloth with bright red threads. Her tireless fingers shuttle between the lace-bands and bone. A scream goes through her as she severs the threads. She pierces the night with her needle, but her blood merely pricks a web of shame. Humming a song that only she knows, she wonders about this rage sewn into her, this weft that makes the scissors blunt as stones.

Seated in darkness, spinning loss after loss as night doubles her stitches, she weaves without end, spins threads dark as clouds.

With no fire in the cabin the day soon became night as the wind banged on the shutters and the rain, furious, lingered in pools before entering the room. She sat waiting, in her shrewd eyes was a sort of refusal, a revolt, and on her milky forehead appeared a sort of venomous calm as she watched sloping shadows fall on the moon soaked pallet which, for years, had forbidden any message except the tale of her defeat. Outside, the dogs sat quivering as night entered the dark fields. Finally she hears him calling out, in fervent braids, the collar of her name, walking across the flooded fields on his way to the cabins. When he enters she flushes crimson and, for a moment, she is hesitant, subdued; in her own way her desires have gone elsewhere, beyond imagining—at the sight of him she finds herself dazzled; the world was white and it had already pierced her, lifting her skirts, branding her profane. But as he steps over the threshold, wearing a look smudged with courtesy, wet and heavy with charm, something tumbled inside of her and she heard her heart collapse… The first blow bloodied his head and eyelid, the second blow forced him to hang his neck down, the third dispossessed him of his strength forcing him to slump onto the pile of skirts, silks, and stockings, his eyes wide and doleful in the lace-work, his mouth opening and closing like a fish caught in a net.

On each intricately knotted thread the image of all that she had lost: and, in the silence disturbed by him, a long lingering word whispered again and again—coming, as it were, after the rain and ashes—a rutting word for the years she lay naked, pinned beneath him, lashed to the spools, weaving a thread of mockery for that which no longer covered him, the force that saw in her the purest of mirrors.

But two questions remain. Did he know, when his conquering hands lifted the veil, what he would discover in her eyes, hanging there by a long black thread? Did her weakness later seem a lesson to her masters, and to him, an essential test leading to their particular consciousness of existence, to the acceptance of a life lived along the slay?

Fields I

I
Out of the low swamps
this hot air blowing, fading away into mist—

II
to hoes to iron to your numbing hands,
this calamitous appetite
time has for living things (a summoning bell):

III
your grandmother awake, fully clothed,
who calls only me the fool,
the basins not yet washed,
the meat not yet tendered,
as you sift the coarse grains of summer,
the virginal vertiginous weight of each instant:
longing for time still.

IV
The nights grow more obscene. Severed thumbs line the window sills.
The stupor of the unliving pours through cracks in the boards. The
stranger who stands at the threshold, who knows whether he feels
shame because of the mold and urine.

V
Resentment walks beside you as your rags flap in the wind. What
stirs in me is the melancholy of the once was. The unlit fires that
have no need of servants or luxuriant houses. The rooms that let the
candles burn as the dark grows deeper year on year. You and I do not
need this yes of solitude. Your delicate hands should not hang like
rocks and stones.

VI
The radiance—it was not long before we saw it in the river, hidden between the cots and stove, beyond the many thresholds of happiness and care. It had neither language nor words. Neither meaning nor loss. It ignored us as a sign of respect. And we just stood there, waiting, our faces blank with cold. Yearning for what we were born.

VII
Go, better spend more time with your family.
Destitute, diminished, forever stammering:
I hunger for the poem still (the resting bell).

The One Way Pendulum

I
I remember one particular summer afternoon when I was playing trains with mama and Melanie said: Someone has come to take your child away and, more softly: these dark tunnels enter the dream like needles or waves. In the house opposite they're rehearsing *Dreams unspool from their contexts*. It's started raining again.

II
My sailboat glides by on the lake (the moment conspicuously insignificant aside from its sad sad beauty). Why? Because the sun reflected every gesture while nothing stirred, the low lying branches nearly unrecorded by time, or was it the plate in my head that began to rustle in all that brightness, allowing the dead white spiders to discover my nature and sense? Beneath the lowest point the word grows colder in the depths, a coldness which, as I entered it, pulses with shame.

III
There are hot and cold moments. That much I can guess. Between there and here I want to remember everything even when it doesn't exist. What is *mine* passes by on the lake, it burns in the light of each reflection. The last carriage edgeless, shirred with cold. Looking as if God had never spoke. Where is Melanie, has she forgot me? Sometimes it's hard to distinguish people from thoughts. That word 'kindling'— when the fires go out, it just turns and slips away. But there's a word that she won't let me leave behind and that is endless in its genesis. What was it, a word so foreign and extravagant it's removed from all alphabets?

IV
I am not here to wallow in conjecture. In the silence of these rooms, someone approaches dazzling. Mummy says all objects are *silly*. Who am I to say any different? There's someone breathing in the darkness. Melanie draws closer and says into its ear: get up, I've come to take you away. The forces that bind us absolute as we sail into a cold sea, the nights cruel beyond reckoning. Somewhere a little alarm goes off. You wake.

Teddy and Me

Walk down this flight of stairs
and let your wishes become sobs,
an angel of glum travail, falling into the haven of what is
where wishes are once more indited.

And walk down the saw
on the burr of things
upon bleeding feet into a world known not
where all feelings are frozen

in an artificial paradise of time off center.
If I knew you were there
I would immolate myself on the hour
and call time on all feelings slain

But like you I am the serene stranger.
Only imagine what is or is going to be,
relearn the loss so that this wish,
that burns in the heart and keeps on falling

becomes another chance, another gesture,
stained from the great ashen clouds
as you fall into the lap of one senseless wish
and stand motionless, waiting for *now* or *never*.

The Red Ribbed Ledges

It is the time of night.
The windows of office blocks shudder with thirst,
and spider webs decay without end,
and fresh snow buries itself on the topmost wires.

It is the time of night
when taxis say no is the only answer,
and what comes to pass in the back alleys
is a lesson in impossibility.

How easy it would be
to deny my eyes and stop my ears,
forget everything. Confess I haven't seen a thing.
What's there to say?

It's not the same world anymore,
I no longer endure my reflection.
My steps are no longer audible.
I have no flesh or skin. Things
no longer wait to be inspected.
The ghosts, plagued by sight,
have vanished before vanishing.
And old soldiers no longer rub
their immaculate missing limbs.

On nights such as these
nothing is alien, nothing but.
The billboards, huge, immovable,
have grown bare as rock.
And the signs, stretched across the sky,
like a line of severed heads,
go unnoticed by chimera.
Maybe a suicide's laughter stirs behind the mask,
but the mask
has crumpled into dust.

There is no need for souvenirs.
No need for time to be unraveled
         into a series of meaningful instants.
Tomorrow eyes will collect the coats of years,
and my secret tongue, waiting in the fields,
will find all that has been lost
brushed down in the stables
    a few feet away from a newborn
abandoned in a call box. Or maybe not.

It is the time of night
when drizzle
arrives like men in uniforms on the high upland hills,
unforgiven but for all that
ever eager for the feeling of being briefly on top.

Or when murderers
turn fiddlers from the tents,
when after each canted pass
the strings can still be heard humming.
Lost between hunger and escape.
What more is there to say?

Me—I've found a simple answer,
have become a figment of myself.
A statue in stone, no longer breathing, carved out of indifference.
As if the letters that I signed and sealed,
written inside each crystal,
have all been absentmindedly erased by an angel.

In any case, my life hangs by a thread,
my creditworthiness
is red. Then black. Black, then red.
A chattel carved out of fire and earth,
with no imprint, or thought,

hope, or delusion,
and no blood to shed upon the rust thick neon.

Into the Pit

From the no-longer
        also silenced
by aphasia and the little tropes
        of blood
he falls
        into dust and sand,
                the birthmark buried
by a daughter
        as she scoops for a signature
                before the ironies
erupt and grow silent again
        where, oh so beautifully grave,
                she checks
him out
        from the memory of his name
                like an old tyre from a steel rim . . .

        Where does the willingness
to yield rise come,
when, packed tight in the quagmire,
everything else feels interred
        already over
                before it begins
and human warmth
        gives way to blackened flesh
that seethes and burns
having been lying there for years,
        burning in the shadow realm
                like exposed legionnaires
                      on the barren slopes
                          of the mirror.

Life means living, yes,
        but how many can live with it,
              fugitives
                      between dream
and desire?
        There are forts and poems
            riddles
that dwarf every ambition
signifying, briefly, before collapsing
        into ossified fragments.
        And yet uncertain as he was,
what animated him most
was the fear of being far apart,
        of not knowing how, even now,
            each form is broken,
                    graveled by a crush of sand
the double jeopardy of devotion and cruelty
the only price
            for the resurrection
                of appearances . . .
it's true—who knows when being here
is simply a portentous whisper
        or merely the echo of simplicity
        collected from exile, the mourned-for origin—

yes, too far apart from her to know
            that the less deceived rises
                    from the depths of the long familiar
even when
        in the deep earth
            we sleep like titans
                blazing beyond the forgotten runes.

The mound is built. The hiding places
have all been witnessed,
       and yet the already known
                is never noticed
     in oblivion's department store.
     An infinitely small storm, an event,
       juts from his eyelids as he sleeps—
but what he seeks,
eating away at
         the edges of his awareness
is separateness,
the quarantine of a wished-for inheritance
forever closed off from her childish creation.

He is a father, a philosopher,
    he has no knowledge
beyond this game of veils.
    As he rises
        neither prophet nor angel
     he shakes the ashes
           free from his feet.
Amidst the silence of the deluge,
         the anguish of the one paternal eye,
how many of us could slice through
the long umbilical threads
smouldering in the ruin, no longer mastered or free?
            Perhaps at Colonus,
when either walking the terrain
of unspeakable anguish
or completing the journey
of an impending death.

Strange how the days anchor her,
    like a poem
        like a new embarking . . . . as if the only surprise
was the delayed noise
    of a scream duly weighted,
        falling
with a stranger's presumption
    on the still inchoate ground,
as if life can only begin
after receipt of the colossus,
    it's outline in pieces, unmade.
        And everything was, and is repeated again.

In his dream,
        the titan has only one eye
but no writing,
    for who needs to read the unfamiliar?
It's a gaze that erases past and future—
it never closes, for only life can close it.
Haunted by blindness to the end: he persists
when everything else falls apart, moves on.
    The unchanged recompense.
        The sun washes her,
enters the bleached glare of the pit.
        He cannot see it
lost in chaos, veiled by dust,
waiting for her to fall,
    sinking,
        helpless at the signals and allusions
            but unable to deny them, the heritage
            filled with insignificance
                like a newly opened cave.

Orphans

Spoken but unheard.
Whatever was thought or said,

these black, mourning sounds
unsleeve the cauls as fetus-gifts,

their crippled being alien,
a litter in the albumen of thought.

Whatever our deformity,
here it is a lost child.

Because we parented the creature,
here ruin is the sign.

VII

Faros

It is the hour of departure, oh unlucky one,
when the ships swallow all number and law.
It is the hour of departure,
deserted like the villages at dawn.

The men were led out first
in single file over a frozen field—
it's hard to tell one from another and whether
if we were them we'd fill the air
with blissful cries, or walk
stricken with the worst evil.
The men came first
with crowds from the ships and taverns, hospitals and parks,
the looks on their faces blotted out
by the multitudes
as they trudge on uncomplaining.

A rage for absolution can be like that:
capricious, deadly, yes, but shrouded by the worst atrocity,
with no marauders
to crank out the reckoning
over salt heaths, scrabland, or moor.
Only murderers then, who after spilling blood
still hammer at the clevis fastened to their necks and feet,
know what it means to be guilty, cast out,
while we, uninjured by the worst, stay as we are,
without remorse, dangerous in our complicity.

The men went out first
with murmurings from the axes and boarhides
and resheafed swords
the suddenly exposed animals on the slopes
and the polearms
begging to be fetched from the raftered barns
standing cold and grey and heavy.
Who could imagine such offering?

The men went out first
to eyes the colour of salt and names to cleanse the earth
and in their shadows
angels fell through trap doors
(into a hole that goes unwitnessed).
The coasts abandoned ... as they gaze out to sea,
waiting for what comes into view:
the sails, or so they believe, that no one can put a name to,
as they abseil over white cliffs
stranded between the fall—
as if the precipice, and the taking leave,
were, to the sea, the same sorrow
as a mirror, so far away,
it no longer knows its reflected life—
and the shape of falling, ended in the endlessly possible.

As if the black slicker of time
edging closer, rushing on,
underlined like words in a ledger, oblivion's closed fist,
were simply there to prevent them
reaching the summit, and so cash in
the irritating malignity of being chosen.
Before this ending the wharves
would rather trail red kerchiefs and flags,
stash away stars to auction. Where rows of hands
spinning in the narrow isles
of the lots—the wildly
erratic constellations so rapidly replicated
every election must become a lottery
for slaughter to immediately ensue in the streets.

The men went out first,
each the other's fear entire, and each
the other's desire to live beyond fear.
The rain incessant and, louder now,

someone screaming,
but not one of them looks back.
Or maybe a voice was heard, but
not one of them understood what was said.
Or maybe someone did look back, but
only because the instant is a rare privilege,
the waves cresting and breaking,
the sea *un*conscious of its end
(the flaw that converts *other* into *victim*):—
the gravest sacrilege
to confuse sheerness of surface
with a sea so godlike
that, viewed from above,
(by those exposed to its emptiness),
it accepts always within itself the unacceptable.

It is the hour of departure,
which the horsemen call out in the boroughs.
It is the hour of departure, oh sleepless one,
mired in the salons at dawn.

The Wolves (Acts I and II)

The forest, wolves white and childless,
and shadows around them, like dark glass.
The deer comes unknowing out of the bracken,
while a brook glides by cold and quiet

and follows dirt roads and grey birds
and a youth slowly dying in the tangled foliage.
Soon a buzzard falls down the gorges—
the flesh cloven, unzipped to the bone.

The nights seem endless in the murk,
burnt villages, empty houses and cars,
and ravens climbing upwards in a starless dark.
A wolf sinks into the drifts, a boy in jeans runs onto the road.

Along the limbs of the trees
wolves sit huddled, watching him,
their eyes like skiffs
washed in snow and all but translucent.

Towards the still-burning town
they lead him, where children are playing,
and the highways are silent,
to a world empty of depth without meaning.

They dig their claws into him.
He tries to shoo them off, but they'll not be shook.
They shuffle along behind him howling with grief.
Their staring eyes rapt for having found him.

❦

I am not like other men.
My hatreds are not yet in speech.
When the day wanes, my blood sounds like a troubled beast.

*Sometimes, at night, my eyes
are like blood-red beads
peeling off trees like ice dissolving—*

*Sometimes, after the rains,
I have come slinking out of the forest,
the flash of my teeth visible in black thickets.*

*My scent purls over the branching streams,
my heart beats quicker in the laurel,
my fur is so thin it no longer matters.*

*A dream-child, of course,
from the higher mountains,
who cries wolf at the blood of war.*

*But my journey
is not from some heart of darkness,
a rime slavering
beyond the rational shores of language,
a noun tearing at throat and vein.*

*Look deep into the eyes of this poem—
do they sparkle with fear or emptiness?
What if the scars of existence
still burns on my lean starveling limbs
do I shrink back from the howling?*

*Flesh without distinction, infinitely so,
but a barrier has fallen
between the animal and its substance.*

*There are no more wolves
to gnaw to dust each symbol or metaphor,
or hunt down every deserted human image.*

*Once I had a voice; now I have silence:
for what I was
the world-to-be is a sheepish apparition.*

*From my mouth emerges a sound
that is no sound, a howl hushed by a miracle,
because of me wolves arrive suddenly, then vanish.*

The Bloods

Infinite in their gentleness, standing akimbo in a pose not even Alighieri could endure: fortified by blood. The rain was coming down in torrents and washed over them, gathering in rivulets on their nakedness. After an interval of weeks, maybe months, they stand there at the limits of what is known and so utterly exhausted, stripped naked at the bivouac fires. A want, as the night sets in and darkness starts to hum in the forests dissembling its encroachment, is not a memory. The world is growing stranger, inexplicable, beyond recognition. Then there is no telling how many desires are being covered up, unowned, unoccupied, hidden. They remember everything—the songs and trees—and the pain submerged in each photograph as they ford the river and the winds waylaid the scows, the words mesmerizing, like music, and perpetual like an echo: so they walked through the heat and dust nearly mad with terror. Walking to what was aired in the hope that others would remember to pronounce their names, lightly and carelessly with their tongues. There is so much to be seen as they tramp on, and so many unanswered questions as they head southwards. A string of raindrops reveals so much emptiness you cannot take it all in, the low dark hills are already hazy in the mist, the words lost amid the chasms, no longer a trace in the landscape. What will it all be like in twenty years' time when you try to remember? Will there have been sunsets rising behind the mountains in the distance? As long as the dead escape by following the path you carved there no one listens to you. Anyways it wasn't meant to be. The journey can only lead to disaster, but what really scares us is not the future—we begin to see our destination as the end of time. There is so much that is menacing, and in the clearing it dawns on you that the whole of creation is a frightful tableau. There ought to be room for other kinds of escape, or baptism. Beyond the deserts and fires and carrion birds—letting what sustains them enter into you just once, and then laughing as the campsites and belongings are burned—if they were patient enough, in their nakedness, to go near the horses and herds. Alas, in the graveyards the dead can no longer be shot or burned—propped up against the cabins all dried and caved as if wearing delicate masks, or left skewered in a dark wood with blankets draped over them—what can one do with such meaninglessness? Nothing human about the heaped and hacked bones and, from the remnants, we know pleasure won't be returned. It is possible that, finally, like coming to the end of a long, dreamless night, there will be new kinds of holiness or sacrifice. A new happiness that grips your mind, a fate that is weighable, as you tip the scales and accept that there is nowhere to go. As if you couldn't quite admit it, yet, that caesura is the meaning of the world just now. Waiting for those unnecessary disguises to be over before the world presents itself as irredeemable war. The charred ruins buckling in the wind—and insisting that words, like *torture* or *truth*, remain empty aside from this insistence. But no one gets to decide. The universe is darkness absolute, a dead glare burning beyond existence. After all, its their command too—the strangers who want not charity but defilement, to be brutally raped and slain. As for hell, everyone could write this, but that's just it, the pathos of this word 'hell', when we can't help thinking that the time for writing it is past. But the drovers—and they in some way understand this differently—it would never occur to them to repeat the mistake, even if they could begin the terrible journey feeling that no one will survive, precisely because they do not want to, feeling grungy from dirty backsides, the cookfires no longer burning. So the epitaph in the outlying buildings is: naked and impregnated, time is *this* meaning, this event. And in its wake, the whole history of the missing person is plastered on the notice boards, next to the military ads in the upper right-hand corner, held up by a rusty nail.

Newborn as Letter C

Another year has passed. I've returned to the place of my birth,
to the enemy whose grin unfolds like dark butterfly wings
in the wilderness
flitting across the alder's yellow eyebrow, or perhaps we are twins
—tormentor, whose bright eyes are the shade of mine, mired in the same
bad blood.

Now Fall Law is abuzz with digging
and hay rope washes in the burn, medusas,
bronze birds, streams of muck,
beasts dripping with spray, the goddess naked,
poultices to bind the womb of creation
for the monster since risen.

The gorge is a pulsing chasm. I can smell his skin
and his inside-out organs. And the charred heart devoured
from its pitch black cavern
as he hunts me through the ice; the wreck of snow
melting us to nothing as day breaks onto storm.

At sunrise, I will loosen some more of his flesh,
drive the point home into the molten cast
pupil, break the large bones. The creature is my echo
and my future. But I am his nightfall, his abandoned grief,
and my scarred surface never heals.

Lakeshore, Trilce

    Ah where to when I feel my life
is already elsewhere, when the stars, having risen,
let their luminosity shudder in the fog,
rousing me with fevers
and the glamour of a last chance.
I'll weep for a second time over this
driving along lakeshore for a faster
ruin—each moment a plasma screen.

    Can I say that I've been betrayed?
Three-fingered the town has closed
its doors, now it edges forward
on cleft heels; every passerby
whispers betrayal on the bluish mountainsides,
        and the summers by the lake
that seemed all the world,
who now could carry me to the other shore?

I am reconciling myself to progress,
I am watching
as the hills of my childhood are blown apart,
the numbers
no sooner held than probate,
and maybe, tomorrow,
a town without rails will await me,
        and the bluish blue hills,
forced to drink down iron,
   will not let the carcinogenic wound
dig further tunnels for the giddy air,
drawn over cliffs into emptiness.

And I hear a whisper that astonishes me,
am I not the wound? sporting
myself as a flawless fire—
a genetic grieving willfulness?

I could build myself a tower,
but could I leap from it
plummeting into the lake, the sudden renunciation?

The rocks glisten like old wallpaper.
Nothing moves near the burnt-out fires.
Nothing resists
the unpredictable, incessant
gods of darkness or decay.
On the great southern shore
the splashing sound of silence
implodes as thunder and lightning
fall on the lake's dark mutating
flesh like a blade: the caves carved out of phosphorus,
the minerals burning briefly into shards as sparks fly.

It was a long time ago
when the sun, glowing white, chased away
eons from memory,
scalding the honey blue granite grey.
A pain reminding me of my defeated childhood.

Tomorrow I shall walk back to myself
along the black crater of the lake.
I shall let life take whatever course it will,
my blood a series of explosions.
Shame and anger will light up the sky,
puncturing a hole for the noonday sirens.
In the random heat haze I shall seek myself,
and stand there just as ruined,
the ashes piled onto wagons,
the wounded taken to whatever is left of the city,
the stink less strong in the rain,
but acrid, metallic,

like the skin of lava,
swart, oozing resin on slaves: free of memory.

☙

In the clearing time stops dead,
the flash, already over, makes me close my eyes,
black healing streams of elixir
stars going out one by one. For ever.
Across the many scattered reaches.

Soultracts

They will die on a boat in the hold. The way lost will not be refound; the pateras will give way to stars and seawater and they will be pitched headlong into immense cold—dying of thirst, hunger, hypothermia. The waves and crosswinds will force them to sack each hose of water, else lie, end to end, in parallel displays of foil luminous on black sand. Their memory will never reach the threshold of loss but will remain in limbo, shoreless in the round, bleached of identity. Theirs is a landing in never: suitcases of silence taken to camps of arrival, sorted into piles of nowhere that quickly pile up, strewn on the side of the road. They need to hurry up for, once again, the waves are full of corpses. Black bloated corpses wearing masks, without shoes on their feet.

November 29, 1781. The disease is spreading very quickly now like a distemper or plague. The men are uneasy and have succumbed to terror of soul; they imagine themselves poisoned, pits of shadow falling across their swollen faces, mouths agape. The doctor has listened to their complaints and advised them. But he won't give them physic because he believes the source of their complaints is not corporeal. The doctor is a better man than I, learned, with abundant gravitas. But he has allowed himself to be open to the niggers--perhaps they have bewitched him? Let history be the judge but this plague is not natural. It is African. The disease took up residence soon after we left the Southern coasts. Perhaps it was already lingering, biding its time as we hauled anchor before beginning its murderous course...

November 30, 1781. The remaining crew stands dripping beneath cloudbursts as storm winds moan in the rigging. Below us, far below us, are huddled groups of blacks torn between self and obligations to others. Women, men, and children forced to jump overboard. Even though we are insured against the loss, some of the men give in to their natural sympathies. The Boatswain has to remind them of where true terror lies. But then I also feel sorrow. It was not enough to curse the plague, or weep for it, for our imaginations have been enslaved. The disease has pierced and emptied us of our old habits of self like a canker of the brain. I couldn't look over the bulwark. It was the Second Mate who told me that the waters closed over the bodies almost instantly, swaddling them. The last thing to be seen: liquid sulfurous eyes looking back at the stern like holes in the water.

November 31, 1781. It has been raining constantly. There is no wind. The skies weigh on our shoulders. The men are terror-stricken. To a man they complain of melancholy and foreboding. Earlier in the day, when I was inspecting charts and provisions, the First Mate, a man I considered almost a friend, confessed to seeing blood-soaked shadows in the hold, of hearing the approach of footfalls where not a body is to be seen. It is not surprising that in the absence of honest endeavors the crew is distracted. I need to talk to them, restore the fretwork.
Last night I dreamt that my heart had been cut open and was dripping black infected blood onto the map table. The Doctor's word for this is disunion of soul; *a sign condensed from nothing and, leaping into nothing, reveals itself.*

Doctor's diary, November 28, 1781. I have spent a restless night, sleep has been intermittent. Such dreams! And always the same one. A slave girl chained in the hold. Laid out like a ledger for the appreciation of her quality. Darkness made visible. Even with a candle I have to strain my eyes to see her. Huge, swift eyes, dark complexion of tone, long lithe limbs, naked. The rest of her face is hidden by a veil, yet I sense the bitter twist in her mouth, her anger and defiance. I go towards her, eager to take possession of this insolence, leash her to my will, but as soon as I come near she disappears into air, evaporating. The light flickers then goes out. As soon as it does so I feel my feet sink into the ground as if I were walking underwater. Salt at the back of my throat and silt in my mouth, the pains in my chest unbearable—breached at the break point. As I am sucked down there is a roaring in my ears and I see traces of speckled gold floating like a cloud which engulfs me . . . When I tell the Captain of my dream he warns me to tend to my duties so as not to be useless to others as well as to myself. 'Remember,' he says. 'The morale of the steed is in the spur of the rider, the slave's in the eye of the master. Never loosen or upturn this harness, or we'll all be buried by revolt.'

What happened next was disquieting . . . The Captain has given me permission to examine him, but I suspect his condition is due to a disordered brain. His attitude to those around him has become fierce, strident, and he is prone to angry outbursts. Certainly there is a meaning there that eludes me: and, vowing to meditate on his stupor, I suggest that he forego any contact with the cargo. 'God preserve us from such contact,' he cries, gripped by a sudden desperation. At such moments he is literally unrecognizable. After he left, I felt an undeniable relief.

The Captain considers the Africans to be the sign—indeed the very essence—of disease. 'They are the chasm,' he says, 'the abyss. When I am near them I am sapped of all being.' I ask him to describe his ailments but as soon as the

Africans are mentioned the same thing happens: language disappears, drifts, sinks into himself; the windows of the mind grow dimmed, no longer able to carry the burden of its weight. Only one figure emerges, in a slightly more articulate image, of pale sirens in the water flowing just beneath us whose darkness is deeper than the night's, urging us on ever onwards; becalmed in a sleep of reason the Captain watches them braid the moonlit waves.

Ship's log. December 22, 1781. We are nearing Port Royal. I have assumed command after Captain Collingwood lost his mind, then his life, at sea. In his final hour he had the look of one hollowed out by despair. The men pitied him for being so reefed. In his last few days all he did was sit up on deck, squinting at the sun. He refused to move until all the shadows had dissolved into early evening. Nightfall with its bleakness gave him no rest and he had to be restrained below decks for his own safety. He could be heard muttering to himself of having seen a shoal of white creatures shearing through the waters just below the surface. Creatures (or illusions?) in whose grasp he hoped for deliverance. At such moments he is wild-eyed and desperate, but nothing ascends in this uncommon ocean.

Atlantis

The sea reeks of them.
Apes on the tideline,
blue-beards, bastards, birds,
startled by black cliffs of water,
the blond spurs
rising and falling
like rusted tins in the steerage,
the young men freed to measure the routes, the remainder.

Look at their eyes
listing, searching for one another
turning themselves into eyes made of oceans,
the one thing held in common separately perishing,
and the sea muttering:
see, this is the end of the road, the last surrender;
what do you see, in a world gone blind with accumulation,
that each is the coin, each the life,
free to drown by prearranged murder?

I know that this is my own
private misery; a glance stolen from the last century.
Here to confess that the cleaners
have left the decks grimy, overrun by empty metal braids ...
I know that there are decisions
harder to return from,
a moment when everything goes wrong,
but here the loss is insurable and, at the end of the trial,
the cargo are wraiths
now and for ever, fungible claims
inside an obituary ark, sued by self-protecting affidavits?

And indeed the ship is a padlocked tower
with rooms inside farther rooms
and where being means seeing too-much in a tiny space.
But for slaves, who will not be remembered, nor praised,

its hard not to gag on the mush
watching the wave-lashed coasts, the dead taken against danger.

Don't think me melancholic,
I have no patience for elegies.
The most I can handle is the sad sad
nothing, and for these islands
I will remain the tattered whisperer of nothings,
ring tone for the voicemail of ex-slaves.

Of course there are other poems:
forms where boats
burn bright in seas aflame,
and where each image
vanishes in celestial fire,
and what does not turn blue is dazzled by the telling.
For the writ is inside the bottle,
tossed beyond danger or hope.
Beyond the less and the least,
and the infinitely small honour of the poem.

And yet what continually amazes me
is this wish to follow the adventure
without weakness, or pause.
e.g. to have the inheritance equal the damnation;
recognise the fates we are.
This wish to leave the coils of home
and go, once more, into new, unheralded depths.
The prow and stern ringing
with the sympathetic cadence of new meanings.

For a slave not all storms are salutary.
And not all fictions are daubed with greasepaint and ocher
wherein we get to plunder with guile or force.
As any slave will tell you, illusions

count for nothing when you're caught.
For whoever drowns here
gasping for air, dragged away by the currents,
will go forth,
floating like mist on the saltscoured scrim,
and all that he will be thinking about
are the very first words (the names)
that he will repeat to the skies—
for repetition brings the named ones near.

As for me, the son of an ex-slave,
all I need to live by is a life without fear,
or pardon, a life where the names
are already spoken without alibi
because the unsaid is not the unsayable.
I am not here to perform
the little drama of *Zong*
along the border marked by confession,
for this is not a game of hide-and-seek.
Even when all the voices are swallowed,
everything remains witnessable.

A slave is the price paid for this rule.
For who could fail to see the ship listing,
the wild birds circling the lees,
the bodies plunged into free fall,
and where they lapse, drift,
the waves crash and darken
as the owned world burns from shore to shore.

VIII

The Art of 000-3

My blindness is not darkness, it is deep snow
and leaves me skittering, like a toboggan, across the ice.
It has crystals and crests, abstract suns, and blizzards.

I have made myself a room from mounds of silence,
so many ice blocks to protect my presence
from the swerving snow whose sightless yearning
has a bitter gleam in it
though in the wilderness
it freezes my footprints, and allows hunters to call my name
on the rafted ice.
At times, during summer,
I have heard the bergs collide
and saw the thin line of the imagination become a chasm
of sliding water, the mountains gone. Word drifts outside my tent,
endless, but like thunder in the distance,
shapeless and without sound.
I don't think I can stand another winter,
the sliding sea is all artifice, and the gulls mimic its roar
as they move far away. I'd like to pull the trigger.
Walk across the thin ice
to the shoals, and touch the nearest before the smell of blood
is made abstract, unreadable,
and the cold fury of the drifts is made white by my lips
looking for prey, searching the pools, masked in the sifted water,
undiscovered, seal cubs bleeding on snow frozen black
by metaphor.
So many of my landmarks have perished in the weather!
The dry speechless ice, abandoned stations, stars, sea-worn vaults,
blue-rutted expeditions at the rim of the world,
the incomprehensible dream of a purer whiteness,
crags of my black love!
I pant in the mists as the hunter crosses the ice and fjords
and trembles, as the transparent night brims under the corona

and leaves us looking at each other,
outside time
and slipping on a frozen earth without meaning. The tides thin out
at the sight of those swelling archipelagoes, as if they are dragon spines!
My blind eyes
signify a deep frost, like pissholes and islands
abandoned to the sea, with storms and westerly winds
and on the glaciers new ice for black speech, buried in silence.

Fields II

I found a footprint in the sand
When I saw it
I grasped, for the first time,
the true weight of my loneliness, because I knew
the imprint could never be mine alone
And I saw, in the trait,
a world ruled by
demons, cannibals and animals wearing masks
I just stood there watching it all just wash away
next to the marshes
as disgust turned into fear and fear into a desire
to live in
a world no longer inhabited, for the measurer,
by definition, is always murderous
It is because of the island,
from the near sea to the high mountains,
everything that is real is vanishing
and bears the blessèd mark
of birds asleep in barbaric trees
Take the two shining eyes, for example—
like lamps on the footpaths
they cast the blackest shadow
and disappear into a grey void dimly flickering
I saw in them
the peril, unease, or despair of the truly menacing
The negroes like gods, but goat-smelling, too—
with dirty feet,
cocks fabled to adoration,
and heads to cushion a word that reigns only in my ear,
a love spoken with signs, down the path into the groves,
veering across the nudities that enshrine them
and the tired lust of an agèd monarch
The hungers I have known!
The blessings that delivered me; that I now deliver!
The anguish

that could never equal the nimble, innocent inventions of nature
or the ears and the lips
ready to feed on the flesh of my being
as I scatter on the graves of ancestors TEN grains of corn
If it was only a dark voice that I heard—
his echo the fellow of my outer voice,
his footmark no more than the sea's returning speech
the meaningless heavings of water against the sandy shore
The evil I know
would never manifest itself in such ghostlier striding
My art never measured itself by the solitary, heathen, and enchanted
spirit of the island,
marker of all the years spent alone.

All of a sudden volcanic fire emblazons the air
Some dark presence
re-illumines the greener shards,
reveals flecks in the enormous geysers,
and inhales the fragrant murmurings of the beach
I stand in the heat of the sun
I return to my fortress
I make my earthenware pots
I am
barren and heart-sore
vainglorious and self-pitying
the sovereign of all somnambulists
I think I am in exile from the western world

Clash City Poets

Yes, grey skies, when the typewriter can only write failure
and the high syllables hiss like rain in
the traps, the indifferences, or sorrows, virtual
and not the pages on the table before us,
the catastrophe endless as the sea. Yes,

the smell of rain in the air,
as water makes the world legible
before the damp wood in a heap at the door
reminds us
of the first moments forever sought, forever lost
the rise and fall
asking to be marked
like the slit ears of a slave.

That part about a choice we can believe in
dying for inertia, when pleasure or arousal
has no scale, like traffic
when every direction is undeserving,
and what will not change is change itself,
wading through the rivers
to the scented reed banks
as rain ponders me like a sister, reckless blood.

How imprisoned we are, how fastened
everywhere scanned
through apertures,
waiting days to sleep
without the means to step into the world
without the strength to escape it
without anything but
a peephole into who we are.

Here, with notebooks in hand,
the rain greets us the way people used to do.

The smell of it receding
on the headland, thick with burnt limbs.
A mishap rejoined to a serviceable truth.

In cinders, also,
as the city covers our footprints,
and we reach the other shore,
soon, the feeling that *beauty*
is never as beautiful as we are now.

That it should have been you, beside me,
and not the ones who betrayed her, the CEO
who stonewalled every question we asked,
the poets who quarrel no more,
the bridesmaids
who sailed
into the black sleep of never land
and listed all the sins,
bringing us down to earth.

In memory of Dambudzo Marechera

Riverflesh

The thing sheds its skin in water
The rivers and evergreens, stars and bees

All is blank:
    a calamitous dream of creation
waiting to be milked

Look, at his mewling mouth
        as a bride throws herself in the river
              and an old man's eyes sink into desert

      Lovers come and go
But the true other is a muscle between forefinger and thumb
        Why avoid his lumbering return
              as he drinks and shakes
        next to the swamps' bubbling essence

From his enamel walk pock marked crowds
priests frightening in their joy, their bulimia
    soldiers
        walking through towns full of children
            for which each is ill-equipped

Look into the mirror's ripped seam
        as a hand trembles in the courtyard
        and a yellow eye
      bursts in the corridor
      and stars run out from the veils
        onto a vibrating string of hematomas

What more can this be but a host of doctors
        a dream without words
      a syllable of millions
            for every devout worker

Nothing coheres:
        words are zeroes
ice storms burning at the end of days
                a history of haemocinema

        flickering on the walls but unnatural:
Where he goes he knows that you will follow
                beyond the innocents.

A Sequel

1.

The world with no evil is evil itself
I burn like a dying sun

The world with no evil is lost to love.
When you look into my past

you see
only

a poor man the worse for drink ...
a man who did not want to be loved.

2.

Why on this morning
is every thing hurled against the glass?
Why at this moment
do you sit there
with your hands on your mouth?
A word,
a sorrow mourned for,
is evil, but when it goes unexpressed
does it thirst for love?
Why on this morning
do you look for sights
unleaving, struck brutally dumb?
The birds are corpses, yes,
look at the window
is this not the substance of love?

3.

I walk
down a path dark as pitch
I go down the path and hear a girl sing
Fine and Mellow
along the path of emptiness and recollection
along the path of reflection and reminiscence

I touch her bruised flesh
I penetrate her with my tongue
I caress her, but not with love or kindness
Thorns for the awaited journey. Vinegar for the uncommon dust

4.

Oh
the glory and the malice
the bodies kept alive by the sacred places
and the leafmeal cleaved
next to burnt out skulls

5.

The world is evil, but it is not evil
What it has are fragments and expectation
What it has are genesis and death
I burn, words burn,
a bonfire of leaves in a wood

I will not go back to the shack
I will drink glass after glass
as if it were holy, I will wipe my face with ashes,
I will close my eyes, and see my wife and child again
I will bury the corpses with love

Lester Young by Washington Square

Some day I shall catch my breath
alone in a dark room with the sky clear, clear.

I shall listen to the radio playing
Pennies from Heaven in the filthy air.

The sky will be washed clean of birds
and a dog will bark just once

amid this song of yearning
as I pass from the world

in my mouth this curious taste.
I shall whisper a word I don't know,

a word that means nothing to me
as it passes from me into the bright world.

A world of desolation as I lie choking
on the damp bed while all the years

enter the history of sleep
and never to come again

except as footnotes to this music
rising in the air.

Loneliness, disaster, gall.
I shall hoard each in this room.

Pay a price I cannot name, and lose all
as light fades on my broken body.

The sudden flight of birds
will leave the sky clear

as they pass from sight, while music rises
on dreams laden with longing

breathless in my ear.

IX

Islanded

I
There is a sentence in the room
and one of us will have to go
at it word by word on the bleak
soul market. Tear a plaything
to shreds. Take a certain pleasure
in seeing the soft syllables ooze
into fleshbuckets as the jawlocks
seep acid-yellow blood, bit by bit
in the yeast. I feel like a kid
in a chocolate factory. Too much sugar
on the lashes, or so it seems, rags
dipped in molasses, washed white
by prices they will never reach.
It is the destiny of speech.
The infinite margin of the
accusative, the humane trading
of the ablative oars: the one
steerage into lightening seas
each to each in port and
the incessant lapping water
salting the immaculate breeds:
new roots to graft, new tongues
for the flesh burning in the fields
other codes and other warnings
even grammar is confined and seized
on a homeland so corrupted
even the radicals quite
literally are cut off at the knees

II
A life stolen and repossessed
the peonies and seeds unfolding
cotton in the air and juniper

rife where judgement is done
to the letter. There is nothing
but curses there, bloodlines
intermingled as sibilants bend
to the drawls, and lilacs linger
by options sold for non-retail.
Sails or phantom stocks on the bay
outsourcing the costs of utterance
to the ocean and the terrible thought
of erasure (ships in old bottles)
and the release from debt compelled by
mortgage, while the value of one's life
sees credit surging on the decks
of apostrophe (the blight not yet spoken).
Spectral servitude, and the cry
of the gulls read against the tides
as we tax each asset on the tip
of the tongue, the loading docks free
but the mind starved of donation,
knowing that it will never be free
beyond the soiled and distant port
the ghosts tacking to sails
in an exclusion zone, without
breezes enough for the thoughts sent
out to it on the last of the islanders,
the sight always affecting, like canvas
billowing in the light of the early sun
not yet in the homeland of language.

Notes

'Black Sunlight'
"little aspen tree": A reference to John Ruskin *Praeterita*, Part II, Chap. IV: 'Fontainbleau' (text from *Works*, Library Edition, Vol. XXXV, 313–315).

'Trueblood'
Trueblood: Character from Ralph Ellison's novel, *Invisible Man*.

'Nothing's Left'
Segismund: A reference to Calderón's play, *La vida es sueño*.

'Venus as a Boy'
The title refers to Luke Sutherland's novel, *Venus as a Boy* (London, 2004).

'An Emblem Book'
Pondus meum amor meus; eo feror, quocunque feror (my weight is my love; it takes me wherever I may go): A reference from Book 13 of Augustine's *Confessions*.

'Fish—Apostrophe'
My heart is all on eyes of fish now, its slavery now is colder: A reference to *The Diaries of John Ruskin*, ed. Joan Evans and John Howard Whitehouse, 3 vols (Oxford, Clarendon Press, 1956–59), 1, p, 255.

'Pot Kettle Black'
what to imitate: A reference to the essay, 'Reader's Lockjaw', by J.H. Prynne, in *Perfect Bound* 5 (1978): 73–77.

'Whittling, a Likeness Without Shade or Shadow'
Slavers: A reference to J.M.W. Turner's magisterial oil, "Slavers Throwing Overboard the Dead and the Dying—Typhoon Coming On".

'CHILD BOY MAN'
boy from the green cabaret: A reference to *The boy from the Green Cabaret tells of his mother: Poems 1965-1968*, by Barry MacSweeney.

'NOTHING PRECIOUS IS SCORNED'
The title is taken from Simone Weil, 'The *Iliad*, or, The Poem of Force'.

'TEDDY AND ME'
A poem for Paddington Bear and Theodor Adorno.

'THE RED RIBBED LEDGES'
The title is taken from Alfred Lord Tennyson's "Maud".

'SOULTRACTS'
November 29, 1781: A reference to the *Zong* incident of 1781 when 132 ill slaves were thrown overboard in the mid-Atlantic.

'ISLANDED'
Section II contains reference to Chapter X of *Narrative of the Life of Frederick Douglas. An American Slave. Written By Himself* (1845)

www.ingramcontent.com/pod-product-compliance
Lightning Source LLC
Chambersburg PA
CBHW031152160426
43193CB00008B/337